The Night Goes On All Night

Noir inspired poems edited by Rick Lupert

The Night Goes On All Night

Copyright © 2011 by Rick Lupert / Ain't Got No Press
Individual poems copyright by their authors.
All rights reserved

Ain't Got No Press

Design and Layout ~ Rick Lupert

Thanks to Suzanne Lummis for bringing the night to the city.

No part of this book may be used or reproduced in any manner whatsoever without written permission from the editor except in the case of brief quotations embodied in critical articles and reviews. For more information or to contact the editor for any reason try:

(818) 904-1021

or

15522 Stagg Street
Van Nuys, CA 91406

or

Rick@PoetrySuperHighway.com

or

PoetrySuperHighway.com

First Edition ~ November, 2011

ISBN: 978-0-9820584-3-5 $10.00

Contents

Noir Metropolis	Suzanne Lummis	4
Social Tale	Mike Cluff	7
Broken Alley	Jack Bowman	8
Neon Vultures	Mehnaz Turner	9
Motel Room with Red Door	Anthony Seidman	10
Panorama City	Brendan Constantine	11
Bakersfield	Douglas Richardson	13
Kids	Eric Tuazon	14
A Palo Alto Contralto is in Love with the Stage Manager of a Bayshore Strip Club	Michael C. Ford	18
two o'clock Sunday	Wyatt Underwood	19
Catholic Hill	Ruth Nolan	20
Dante's Encino	Elizabeth Iannaci	21
My Right Arm	Joelle Hannah	23
Hollywood, North	Kristoffer Huelgas	25
B and W	Wanda VanHoy Smith	26
Another Suburban Romance	Mike Cluff	27
Motel Room with Door Painted Black	Anthony Seidman	29
Urban Skies (a dark wave song)	Marc Olmsted	30
Before E-mail	Florence Weinberger	31
A New Town	Douglas Richardson	32
Boulevard	Lady G	33
What the Room was Doing in 1962	Eric Steineger	35
Fritz Lang	Michael C. Ford	36
I need air	Eric Tuazon	37
Reflection	Mike Daily	41
The Sun Takes Us Away	Kevin Patrick Sullivan	42
Look Here, Sister! No, you look.	Peggy Dobreer	43
Nite Life: Heat	Anthony Seidman	44
Reading Hammet with Laurel Ann Bogen	Jerry Garcia	45
Sneaker on a Slick Scrawl of Telephone Wire	Angela Peñaredondo	47
Green Dahlia	E. Amato	48
Nocturnal Activity	Eric Steineger	50
Contributors		51
Acknowledgements		55

Noir Metropolis:

Noir exists, at least in a latent stage, wherever there's a presence of more than 183 people, even if it's a tropical sandbar or stretch of arctic terrain, but Los Angeles is the ultimate noir city. This is true not only because it's given rise to the quintessential noir film, "Double Indemnity," and the quintessential post noir film, "Chinatown," inspired by the treachery and subterfuge behind the development of the San Fernando Valley. And it's true not only because of legacy of Raymond Chandler (who might have been nearly as brilliant in any city -- but not quite, because Los Angeles acted upon his imagination like no other place.) It's because noir loves paradox, and there is no more paradoxical place than L.A. All this sunshine, optimism and shiny hope. All these notorious murders: The Black Dahlia, The Sleepy Lagoon Murder, The Hillside Strangler, the Night Stalker . . . All this promise. All this historical corruption (a long interesting list). All these aspiring talents bursting their hearts on their own dreams like surf on the rocks. (That's a pretty mediocre line of poetry, but, well -- that's what ya get for a nickel.)

Suzanne Lummis

"I want you to do something. I want you to get yourself out of the bed, and get over to the window and scream as loud as you can. Otherwise you only have another three minutes to live."

> Henry Stevenson as played by Burt Lancaster
> Sorry, Wrong Number (1948)

"How I detest the dawn. The grass always looks like it's been left out all night."

> Hardy Cathcart as played by Clifton Webb
> The Dark Corner (1956)

"The streets were dark with something more than night."

> Raymond Chandler

Social Tale by Mike Cluff

Tall suited in bow tie and braces
shoots many bullets into the crowd's faces
a goodly number finally see the sky
for the first time with clouded eye.
He straightens his tight garters and right sock
aims again at the scattering flock
his shirt and pleated slacks are stainless, free
no spots from viscera, pus and brain debris.

Late on in the day
his identical twin takes him away.

Broken Alley by Jack Bowman

The wind whips on Ventura blows up yesterday's Times and
LA X-Press into the street to mix with La Opinion
and Styrofoam symbolism

the old Borders Books stands silent, inside:
crack kids and gangbangers scrawl their tribal angst
onto cold walls in the dark

a soccer Mom feeds more change into the meter
and runs back across Balboa to hook up with
the insurance guy at the Sidewinder Motel

on Thursday next, the coroner heads up "the 5"
from Mission on a long bumper to bumper journey
to the local lock up in Van Nuys, make shift morgue downstairs,

Detective Wilson brushes crumbs from his jacket
watches the exam with vague interest
answers questions, she was found in an alley behind a city dumpster

she had been shopping on the boulevard and then met up with
    the assailant
for some B&D before her eyes were given that stippling pattern
and her throat was closed forever

4th victim, no prints, fake name in the Hotel register,
another mask to uncover
another night in the valley.

Neon Vultures by Mehnaz Turner

Summer in Los Angeles, and the city's covered
my shoulders in mosquito bites. The air's so
thick I could cut up slices to refrigerate. My mood's
not deliberate. Every time I step out of my apartment,
someone hands me a shot glass. Sometimes I wanna
say, do I look like a broad who needs to lighten
up? I wear fishnets under my jeans. On Monday
mornings, the cars wheel heavily down the freeway's
length. I blink back the glances of predators.
Like a newspaper headline, my hopes reek wrath.
And in downtown or Venice, no matter how much
red I wear, I'm a picture cropped in gray and black.
Touch my neck. You'll find it's charged with light.
Still, mosquitoes slip through the cracks, find a way
to bite into my wine-rich skin. Drunk and dizzy on blood,
they travel back down Sunset, past the bars and taco stands,
to the Laundromat on Vermont, where insomniacs
count quarters after midnight. My fortune teller says,
this place feeds on a woman's flesh. Burn your
novels. Drink tequila. Streak your hair orange.
When people ask you what you do, say, I just try
to mesh. The truth is, the city waits for the right
moment to knock you up before it runs you over.
Even the cops and gangsters fall prey to chance.
If you're lucky, you'll miss the neon vultures trying
to hook you in at every street corner. Summer doesn't
end for months. The sun's a crab scuttling across
the shores of Malibu, watching thieves and pickpockets
surf the streets. If you've got the guts, score a gun.
These hard boiled days, luck can't be bought
for a few dimes at the thrift store on Vineland.

Motel Room with Red Door by Anthony Seidman

This is where I boil *Top Ramen* on a kitchenette's stove. This is where I sit reading Ritsos and his doxology: *praise the sun that cannot be burned*. Nightfall, I pace the room: the television newscaster recites the daily famine and fads with the encouraging pitch of a Pilates coach. Hours later, I pull back the sheets, and I stretch out in bed. This is the room with a red door, where every night I struggle, as my Mistress of Insomnia mounts me, pins my arms in between her thighs, then stitches my eyelids open, thread spooled from embers, needle chipped from ice.

Panorama City by Brendan Constantine

We never saw the mountains. They were behind
the General Motors plant and we seldom walked
that far.
        The cocaine boys on Blythe Street were
as close as we got. I don't remember seeing any
birds there. The trees had no leaves & stood
like junkies petrified in the moment of loosing
all their green.
        Shade was in your house or your Chevy
so that's where we stayed. We had reason
to believe the sun was a fink.
        One summer, I let it
look me in the eye & it tried to make a deal.
I was about to shake on it when you pulled me
into the car & yelled into my face,

    ALWAYS ASK TO SEE THE MONEY!

I was too ashamed to nod, but I understood:
the moon was our only friend in heaven.
It wasn't even rush hour.
        We started wearing
dark glasses between the house & the garage.
Panorama City had no view; from any window
we saw another window.
        So we drew the curtains
& called it Privacy. We wore our dark glasses
indoors and called Mood Lighting. We took
dark pills & discovered our natural habitat.

The house became a forbidden zoo. Our eyes
became black & enormous. Chain-smoking
panda bears, scratching our backs on an empty
refrigerator; we never saw the mountains, but
we did know where they were.
        The General Motors plant is empty.
The cocaine boys are all dead. Or men. We don't

live there anymore; we've evolved. I've shed
my glasses & my eyes are smaller.
                          I live in a city
where the trees have cheaper addictions; they can
afford birds. I never see you. I don't know where
you are, but I can guess.
                          You are nearer the mountains,
perhaps in them. You're someplace high, where
you can see the sun coming
                          from a long way off.

Bakersfield by Douglas Richardson

One morning I opened the newspaper
and saw the doe eyes of a drifter
who had passed away
on the side of a highway
near Bakersfield.

The photo had been taken
two years earlier
and was the last known
image of the man.

I never spoke again
for the rest of my days,
which really wasn't much of a feat
since I only lived another week.

When I was alive, I would have
passed him by with mean eyes.

This hurts my core even now.

I am desperate to find this man.

A newspaper blowing along the highway
in Bakersfield
means I am looking.

Kids by Eric Tuazon

These big men,
two tellers,
came into Gil's
and had the strangest
conversation I ever
heard of.

Gil's got a new job.
Works the counter
some place they do
sandwiches. A hole-
in-the-wall place
down Reseda.

It's a living
and sometimes
Gil'll hear things
like this.

The two men
ask Gil for two
roast beef sandwiches
on white with everything
on 'em and get
to talking while
he does them up.

The first man,
the older, balding one,
starts telling
the second one
about a dream.

What about the dream,
the second one asks.
He looked a little younger,
sharper, Gil said.

Then the first one says,
I don't know, it just shook me.
The second one,
the sharper one,
won't let it end with that
and asks, ok, now,
what's it about then?

The first man gives
Gil a look, watches him
cut their meat in the slicer
a couple of seconds
before he gets to it.
The first man turns
back to the second
and gives it.

I dreamt I was playing
with these *dead bodies*—
I don't know, he says.
By then Gil is carrying over
the meat to some open
slices of bread.

The second one goes
with it. Gil didn't see
his face but he goes with it.
What, explain.

The first man goes on.
I don't know, there
were these two dead
bodies. I wasn't doing
anything funny with 'em,
I was just sitting them
up with each other.

By this time, Gil's
putting on the cheese.
they got three kinds

there and if you ask
for everything they
put a slice of each.

The second man
doesn't laugh, he asks
more, he's serious about it.
Sitting 'em where,
what do they look like?

The first man
keeps going. I was
putting them in chairs,
this young boy and girl.
It wasn't anything funny.
I was just putting them there.

He looks at Gil start
putting on the lettuce
and continues.

And I think you were
There, behind me.
yeah, I knew it was
you because I could
see the back of your head.

The second one coughs,
says, what, I thought I was
behind you, how could
you see the back of my head,
why the hell am I there?

The first man's voice gets
louder. I don't know, he says,
you're behind me, and I know
it's you because of the back
of your head, and we're there
setting up these dead kids
on a couple of chairs.

Hey, the second man quickly
yells, that's all you, I don't
have anything to do with that!

The first man shakes his head
as Gil wraps up the sandwiches.
He reaches into his pocket
and pulls out his wallet.
Hey, he says, it's just a dream.

The second one starts pulling
out his own. He looks
at the sandwiches enter
the paper bags,
Gil start to enter their
total into the register.

There's just something
wrong with it, he says,
if you think about it,
there's nothing
decent to it at all.

A Palo Alto Contralto is in Love with the Stage Manager of a Bayshore Strip Club

by Michael C. Ford

Her feelings
for him
were as warm as a
1955 Buick Special
convertible
recently gutted
by fire
over on
Middlefield

two o'clock Sunday by Wyatt Underwood

so Johnny played piano
and played it well enough
that Moe kept paying him
every Sunday morning
about two o'clock
when the week's customers
had all gone home
enough for for him to buy
rent and groceries for a week
and once Moe fronted Johnny
enough for new shoes
and sometimes Johnny sang
and more people stopped talking
for his singing than for his playing
and a girl sat down beside him
and Johnny fell in love
but Moe warned him
against loving his daughter
but the girl told Johnny
not to worry, so he didn't
he played for her and he sang for her
until the Sunday morning
Moe didn't pay but shot him
and Johnny lay so still
so very still
thunder rolled and rain fell
until the girl came out and told him
Moe's gun had held blanks
and Johnny looked confused
"then I'm not dead?"
"only to Moe," she said

Catholic Hill by Ruth Nolan

She handed me a mirrored butcher knife.
Then came the nun-chucks, a fifth of Vodka.

My hair was still wrapped in the French braid
knotted with her strong fingers the day before
while I was teaching my high school English class.

She had removed her long red nails to work on me.
She said she planned to stab her mother in the back,
so I drove her out into the desert after school.
We hiked the mountain behind my parents' house.

The old cross was still lodged into the rocks at top,
my name, carved at 13 with a kitchen knife, still there.

It had been many years since I'd last been here.
I could still see my parents' house, I wondered
how easy it would be for one of us to slip and fall.
At school, she had confided in her journal to me

that she'd thrown a desk at a mean librarian,
that she'd lived in a crack house South Central LA,
that she'd already had four abortions, many dads.
I wanted to give her a gift—an old Geiger counter,

maybe the rattle or papery skin of a dead snake,
a bracelet of rusty barbed wire from a crippled fence,
a memento of the school year we spent together.
Instead, she carved her gang name on the cross,

told me that when she grows up,
she wants to fix hair for the dead.

Dante's Encino by Elizabeth Iannaci

Air hangs rose-rust, the color
of a Cosmopolitan. A fog of tail-lights
merges with the boron buzz
of non-stop shops. Neon's boiling point
is significantly lower than nitrogen. On this

side of the hill, fast boys
lean into the rolled-down windows of slow
cars, let loose expensive smiles
and fat joints. Nothing free
on this side of the hill. Girls

line their eyes with midnight, squeeze
into half-a-dress: circle strangers
on the boulevard; ask for a light. Only
the crazy or desperate continue
to do that which brings them no joy. Inside

an
 apartment compound, the daughter of a feminist
is a Playboy model, aspiring to Centerfold
status: air-brushed thighs, Vaselined lips,
her mother's bootstraps be damned. She believes
her dead father would be proud. A slate-

shirted neo-tech with hair at stiff attention,
uses the glow from his cell phone

to search for what he's lost, sniffs
at the Mustang idling behind him, someone
always waiting to take your space. After meetings

abstainers cluster, drink designer coffee
& smoke under yellow marquees that pulse
Liquor& Spirits.

A denimed & booted
regular insists the world is not
round, but flat & tiered.

A bag-lady who lives in the willow behind
Ralph's market still has a few
teeth that claim she was once
a city-councilwoman. She knows birds
do not sleep in their nests.

Pink is this year's
brown which was last
year's gray, which was the year
before's black. God
save us all.

My Right Arm by Joelle Hannah

With the imminent
mist above our heads,
we smile, convincing
masks, not convincing
enough. At the slightest
recognition, one
slip from behind our
disguises, the midst
falls, heavy, dark, and

suffocating.
I hate you, he says
The mist envelopes me,
strangles me.

My teenage son
burns a wall of
fire between us.
Just stay out of my life.
I reach out to touch him,
I love you, I say,
but the fire bites
at my fingers, scolding them,
Yeah? he says, *Well, I hate you.*
raising blisters
that will take months to heal.

One Halloween night,
several years ago,
I lost him in the park.
As the sun disappeared
behind the trees, the
forest swelled, stretching
jagged, sharp shadows
across the ground, devouring
everything in its way,
including my son.

When I turned around
to count heads I found
one missing.

I considered the forest
for it seemed to sneer,
snicker at my misery.
The forest, cruel joker,
continued to poke fun,
to keep me guessing
until I pounded my fist upon
the ground and cried, *Uncle!*
Only then, did the forest cough
him up and a down pour
of relief saturated me.

But there is no water
to be had in this Sahara.
A dry, hot desert
separates us.
I love you, I say again.
I love you like I love my right arm.
I want to diffuse
the fire but my words only feed it.
Well, he snaps back, *learn*
to use your left.

I know,
I know that this time
he'll have to find himself.
For now, my pen stumbles across this page
because my left still longs for my right.

Hollywood, North by Kristoffer Huelgas

the streets sound like applause
flip flop slap echoes, family tree parades:
children out of strollers pushing strollers full of children,
child spectres on pilgrimage between bus shelters
to the 2AM Orange Line,

emergence
headlights like the drunken eyes on a prom queen
grow apart when they get close to you, become a
········pair of bicyclists instead, roll off the bike lane
into the liquor store parking lots, adjacent alleys,
········through the parks
on the overpass,
········Shooting stars lost in the night, celestial flies
········banging themselves tirelessly against panes of
········smog and ozone

my car had stalled, or maybe blown a tire
in a nail-filled pothole, gnarled, gaping
jagged as they are
········who can remember
I thought I saw it all in perfect ominous sepia
like the streetlights had cast the city as villain in a movie about
itself

the truth of the place:
lines of invisible prose surrounding an old-woman,
cradling a bundle in her arms, stepping in and out
of existence
on approach via lamp flicker and neon sign
growing grizzled till what once was a child is not,
rather,
one of a shopping cart-many sacks of bottles and cans,
old newspapers in grey
with headlines crying out for tomorrow.

B and W by Wanda VanHoy Smith

A sailor told me there are only two colors
to paint a boat, black or white
and only a damn fool would paint one black.
But the greatest movies of all include
Ship of Fools in black and white until in
Hollywood fashion some fool decided to
brighten them with pastel shades of pink and green.
The French recognize America's unique art form
of shadows and light and name it film noir
which gives the impression that black and white
movies are foreign films.
However Hollywood produced classic Casablanca.
Americans knew nothing about expressionism.
We only knew Humphrey Bogart was hot
Ingrid Bergman lovely and Peter Lorre creepy.
We watch character actors like Tracy. Cagney and
Edward G. Robinson not cute like Robert Redford.
George Cloonie is too handsome and tall to be in the
Maltese Falcon.
On the silver screen Boggie was big as life and terrific
and Vincent Price's black fly transformation horrific.

Technicolor took MGM out of the dark ages
but that is neither here noir there
Nothing is ever completely black and white,
not with Ted Turner at the helm.

Another Suburban Romance by Mike Cluff

I.

Brenda always drove by
Court and Westmonte
just to glimpse

Angus waiting for the bus
he was in tweed and wingtips
elbow patched sometimes

like her dad.

She felt the same
about them both.

One day,
her car breaks down
near Angus' seat.

Later,
his black dress pants
with pleats and wallet
is found to the north.

His blue tie
to the south

and his underwear
on a flagpole
at Sparks Middle School
in the east.

II.

And in the West,
Angus now motors
her car to work
while she sleeps.

His shirts are better-pressed
shoes polished
hair stylish
while she still sleeps.

Last week he shot past
a corner
where Jaenine
stood looking for a ride.

She resembles Brenda
but from only a distance
and was

her image
her attitude
her logic
her....

up close.

Motel Room with Door Painted Black
by Anthony Seidman

Past midnight, I sat awake and looking out my window, when a sedan pulled into the parking space in front of that black door. A shadow, carrying a duffel bag, walked into his room, then locked the door. Later, much later, when all of the motel denizens were done watching cable television's bonanza stampedes, fedoras, and twilight ghouls flickering against walls and drapes, I bolted upright in bed after hearing a shot. In the morning, detectives found the corpse, bloody corolla on pillow with black center hole, and which had been pressed over his face; duffel bag gone, no leads, no witnesses, and only the stiff composure of the dead.

Urban Skies (a dark wave song)
by Marc Olmsted

Phone call came on Wednesday
dead body by the pool
cracked glass on the driveway
bikini had me fooled

I reached for ice-cold bourbon
my .45 was drawn
Jake slumped in the corner
half his face was gone

mysteries seldom answered
crimes so rarely solved
the clue is in the cancer
you don't wanna get involved

Here's Leon, one-armed newsie
just tryin' to make his wage
says we all will feel the heat
in this all too modern age

we all will breathe gray air
beneath these urban skies
we all will see L.A. through
Raymond Chandler eyes ~

Before E-mail by Florence Weinberger

Dustin Hoffman asks Warren Beatty
"Theoretically, is there any woman on the planet
that you would not fuck?"
Beatty ponders, then replies "No."
The news never gets to my mail box.
A man who desires us
from adolescence to senescence,
from insatiable lust to a dollop of lubricant?
I would have thrown in a carnal dinner,
chicken soup studded with bits of succulent marrow.
A brisket steeped in red wine.

A New Town by Douglas Richardson

In the city I searched
for a solitary painting,
a rain-blackened tree.
I held hot water in a paper cup,
avoided the hostile eyes of strangers.
Later I left town.
Long grass grew in the gravel
and made the sky turn gray.
Tar on telephone poles –
warm to the touch.
And then open desert.
Transmission towers stretched
into the distance,
past where I could see.
And then night –
almost black, with no mind.
Sleep was the strange night event.
Later I arrived in a new town.

Boulevard by Lady G

Noticed the slim skirt
Standing solo on
On the corner
Windblown

She screamed
Like the back tires
Of a getaway Packard
Rounding Vine

I ran
She fell
Into the tan
Concrete gutter

I grabbed
She slapped
Hats askew
Hers, mine

Easy, doll face
She wasn't, I lied
But it stopped
The slappin'

She lifted the powdered face
Two scarlet lips
Too much rouge
She smelled of booze

Something wrong?
Anything I can do?
Hoped I could
Hoped I couldn't

I,I,I,I
Gotta make tracks to him

Her claw grasped a red hat
Stain on the brim

I'd never know her spirit host
Done my bit
Lucky lit
And I suck in my own ghost

What the Room was Doing in 1962
by Eric Steineger

At first we gathered on the liver green carpet.
It was quiet as lint in the front room,
and we all seemed to be chosen at random
like those dummies on *Ed Sullivan*.
The TV kept rolling its eyes but saying nothing.

Finally a woman announced "Say, what have you heard
about this Cuba business?"
I interred a lengthy riposte before
"Buy a bomb shelter," blurted a man.
The room rapidly filled up with the smoke
of different ads.

Acutely aware of time's slipperiness,
the room found gin in the kitchen.
I got to know all the names:
Bobbi, Leigh, another Leigh,
but this one wore a fetching blue skirt.
She kept blocking my gaze with her compact.

Then Cartwright was working the room talking baseball.
It was brilliant. Exhausted from flirting,
I had parked back on the sofa when
"What do you mean you don't like baseball?
What kind of commie are you?"
Turns out he knew Bobbi from school.

Later we peaked through the kitchen window
to find our hostess passed out in the grass.
The room was in full swing now.
Everyone was laughing; it was really swell,
going out back, positioning her to one side,
and putting a blanket over her. After some pointing,
Leigh knocked over a sundial, so I threw up in the pool.
We got married the following year.

Fritz Lang by Michael C. Ford

> *Danger and chaos: the true*
> *muses an artist must court.*
> -Robert Rauschenberg

He was the 2-headed hydra of cinema: one
for erotica and one for chaos, as they align
with incarceration in a Purgatorial myth of
images on Scarlet Street.

He's the downhill delivery truck that lost
its brakes on a mysterious grapevine.

He's the inebriated Saint Bernard
rescuing actors in the snowbound
mountains of marooned celluloid.

He's an innocent tourist on the
hijacked Hollywood jetliner.

He's a dangerous desert mirage
fearfully in favor of audiences who
have too many empty canteens.

He's mic-booms and lens zooms inside
clandestine and chaotic candle-lit
redemptive expressionist Noir.

He's a German urn full of the cremated
ashes of burnt visions of film-makers
that he swears were, once, living.

I need air by Eric Tuazon

I.

We sat on the edge
of the bed. Beyond
that was the dead

possum, beaten
to death. I got up
and closed
the sliding door.
I put down the bat.

Don't put down
the bat! She said.
Why?
I picked it up.
You'll get blood
on the carpet
You Fuck,
She hissed.

There's already
blood on the carpet.
It's everywhere, I told her.

She smothered her face
in her hands. She got up.
She knelt down.
She was beside it.
She was upset,
 she was saying,
I don't even know
what I'm supposed to do
with this.

I came close. I bent a knee.

Its mouth and its eyes were
open. God, look at those
teeth! I reached out.
She flinched.

Robert, don't, God.
I touched its tail. Jesus!
I picked it up.

Something fell out.

II.

In the morning,
I made eggs but we didn't
eat them. Nancy called
the cleaner. I read
the newspaper.

She hung up, said, A hundred
dollar job, Rob.
A hundred?
One hundred dollars.

I closed the paper.
Damn.
Damn right!
We looked at it.

It was upside down,
lying on pieces of
itself. It made
a new line of color
on the carpet.
It began to smell.
I opened the paper again
and she started saying,
Jesus, Robert, and took it
from my hands and threw it.

It fell apart.
Why did you have to
do that!? God Nancy,
I got up, God!

I opened the sliding
door. She pushed off
the bed. What are
you doing, what if there's
more? It stinks Nancy,
I need air! God, just stay
outside and close the damn
door then, Rob. Fuck!

I slid the door closed.
God damn, a hundred dollars,
God Jesus.

III.

When the cleaner came,
I watched him pick the body
up and everything else
with his hands.

He placed everything
in a bag and closed it.
He went out of the room.
Nancy followed him.

I looked at the stain
through the sliding
door. I picked up
my bat and took
a swing at the air.

Later, he came back
with his equipment.
He worked at the stain.

Nancy came around
with coffee. I took one
and we watched him
pick that up too.
I could see it
bleed and pant,
still in the night,
like two lamp posts.

Reflection by Mike Daily

"Dad, something looks kind of funny here."

"What is it?"

"Your bed looks like it's outside. Your whole *room* looks like it's outside!"

"Why?"

"Because I see the reflection of it."

"Ah."

"I don't think it would be fun to have your room outside."

"Why?"

"Because you will be cold!"

The Sun Takes Us Away by Kevin Patrick Sullivan

I cruised into town
Under a slip of a moon
Highway 1 - a dream's door
Opening in Malibu
But I stayed focused
Stealing myself from the pleasures
Along the Santa Monica Coast and Pier
The blue Pacific lit and glittering
Close to the beach just black
Beyond the light's reach
Oh! this night in L.A. is hot - a Diablo wind
Blowing off shore parches my throat
I stop at the Rose Café one of the many possible
EMERGENCY EXITS
I'm on my way to Beyond Baroque
To read with Landis Everson
But not this night
He cancelled
Suffering a stroke in Boston
As if a RED SNOW FENCE blocked his speech
I read a couple of his poems that night from
EVERYTHING PRESERVED I'll leave THESE MIRRORS PROVE IT
After all this is just
A LITTLE TRAVEL STORY.

Look Here, Sister!
No, you look. by Peggy Dobreer

The bodies were found accidentally
just after 3 am. No one was necessarily looking.
Garth Ave unfolded in headlamps looking north,
From the day she bought that stucco duplex,
she knew everything was going to change.
Stippled between branches of wisteria
he was visible through the portico,
waist to neck, she from hips to nose.

On the slick alley behind the yard,
live wires added static. Sam was
pleated pin stripes and doused in cologne,
collar propped up high above keyboard wingtips.
He had a dangerous bent.
Sam was a man spitting in the wind
and thinking he could always come up smelling clean.

Ha! Sam liked to hum Mac the Knife in a smoky voice.
The sepia of arrogance oozed through his tone
and made her blush. Still,
she pulled an ivory pistol from her pocket,
stood there silenced by her velvet deed,
the hood of her cape disguising her frame,
shrouding a throaty wince at the pooling stain.

Nite Life: Heat by Anthony Seidman

Past midnight, I open the window and stare at the parking lot. Cats scatter, re-group; they claw at each other, chase and overtake each other. Their cries are almost human, almost siren-like; I, too, feel my pores open, and sweat. Electricity frazzles the air, and my nerves chew at my skin, my pulse quickens. I lick chapped lips, and think how this noise will last for hours. I bite my thick lip, taste nickel and tremble with the urge to bite, cry, or at the very least, commit arson.

Reading Hammet
with Laurel Ann Bogen by Jerry Garcia

A red hem swings
hair tousles
a story told

Tall tales
of sweeping Noir

She talks the talk of 1920 Los Angeles
City of her angels
Red cars full of boys
who do their business
in the dishonesty trade.

"The girl took too much junk"
says the flannelled dick
"Hadda smacker out of it"

It's that kind of house
with a parlor
where dames wear silk nylon
and plat-formed heels
they damage wooden floors
and Persian rugs.

Eyes like a fawn
follow every man
who might have a gun
in his pocket.

The girls pass out
revived by salts
they slap and squeal
they all want to tell
their story
to the honking big PI

who's just as honest
as his J.C. Penney's suit
and even dumber
than her fake blonde locks.

Cigarette smoke
and bourbon breath
street light sprits
on detective specs
sweat beads
on the man in shadows.

Diamonds
glint in the grass
of matrons galore
a job too well done
is a curse.

It's a curse.

Sneaker on a Slick
Scrawl of Telephone Wire by Angela Peñaredondo

left behind.
An inky blot,
a black eye on a pale
horizon, no longer hotfooting
on the grease asphalt,
a smear dancing
over the scurries of heads,
a smudge above your eye line
at the end of the day.
Trouble fastened me here
but I don't ask why anymore.
From up here, see men
in their armored stride,
fast talkin', breath puffin'
smoke stacks of business.
I watch the nightwalkers'
hunt for bread,
and the lonely
with their ghosts.
Sirens flare louder,
their strobes gathering
below in frantic flashes,
wheels run over tossed bits
of fast food, stryofoam
and fragmented bottles.
The glass crushed into
tinier green crystals
with each black boot—
a low and familiar crunch.
Like a fishhook in your memory,
my simple short life swings
above the clank and gutter
till someone yanks me down.

Green Dahlia by E. Amato

smacked lips looked
her over like she was
a gangrene cupcake
knew he was gonna eat her
knew it would make him sick

her with her swirls of green icing
her peaks and grooves
her soft landing
her fluff

he wanted to bite into her
all 3 days of no shower and shave of him
he wanted to eat her with only his fangs
he wanted her crumbs under his fingernails
then pick his teeth

he didn't want her to survive this
he didn't think all the way about her poisons
he only knew she was temptress
seductress she was calling to him
screaming for him
harlot baked to die on his tongue
his hot beer and cigarette breath
the last thing she would ever smell

he knew he knew her like that
was sure of it
would stake her life on it.

ravenous he believes her dirty sexy
calls her slut as he peels back paper ruffle
from decaying green food colouring flesh
she auction blocked harlot to feed grim appetites
has no choice but to die ugly drowned in acid

he craves her with stingy stained hands

reduces her back to ingredients heats her sugar
on tarnished spoon til it runs brown alchemy
fix into his vein teeth grit against saturating
jolting transcendence of blissful consumptive
violence

already he wants to bake her again
in his own filthy image
his green dahlia
she deserves exactly what she gets

see
he could tell
just by looking at her
what kind of a girl she was

she wasn't the first;
can't be the last,
but she was a good one.

Nocturnal Activity by Eric Steineger

If I cannot sleep, she knows I will fly.
There is too much to report on out there.

I climb out contortionist.
Grope for my clothes in the upside-down room.
Kiss and escape.

Down the dirt path, unlatch the wood, and into the street.
No one is out.

The night goes on all night.

Contributors

E. Amato's first poetry collection, *Swimming Through Amber*, was published in 2010 (Zesty Pubs). In 2007, she made her international debut at the Festival Fringe Edinburgh, earning 2 consecutive years. A member of the 2011 LA Slam Team, she also represented as a storm poet at WOWps.

Jack Bowman was born to a workin' class family in southwestern Ohio, but soon moved to southern California where he lives today. Changes in subculture as well as the 'spirit of the times' affected his writing and philosophy.His work in the mental health field since 1984, as well as his own bizarre life experiences, figure prominently in his poetry,art, songs and prose. Jack is a licensed Psychotherapist in the Los Angeles area. He has been a published poet since 1991.

Mike Cluff is a full-time English and Creative Writing instructor at Norco College in southern California. His forthcoming book *Elegant Worry* is scheduled to be published in late 2011. He has recently been published in *Sparkbright, The Inlandia Journal, The San Gabriel Valley Poetry Quarterly* and *The Toucan Magazine.*

Brendan Constantine is a poet based in Hollywood. His work has appeared in *Ploughshares, FIELD, Ninth Letter* and other journals. His most recent collection is *Birthday Girl With Possum*, (2011 Write Bloody Press). Mr. Constantine teaches poetry at the Windward School and Loyola Marymount University Extension in west Los Angeles.

Mike Daily is a novelist, journalist and spoken words performer in Portland, Oregon.

Peggy Dobreer came to poetry by way of dance, hanging on trapezes and experimental theatre. Her poems have been included in *Everything About You Is Beautiful,* and *Literary Angles, the San Pedro River Review, Malpais Review,* and *L.A. Yoga Magazine.* Peggy founded the Poetry Series at LMU Extension in 2008, where she coordinates the Literary Arts Program.

Michael C. Ford's last four volumes are out of the *Ion Drive Publishing* catalogue: *To Kiss The Blood Off Our Hands, The Demented Chauffeur, Las Vegas Quartet* and *San Joaquin County Solutions*: this last title being a collaborative effort with text by the author and what resembles black and white movie stills by Sacramento Delta prize-winning photo-journalist Rose Albano.

Lady G is the performance name of **Gloria Oehrlein Derge**. Published in Midwest regional media, she has been living poetry all of her life. Originally from Wisconsin, she has lived in sunny CA most of her life. She has one chapbook *Patches*. She writes of love, loss and hope and the joy of life.

Jerry Garcia is a poet, photographer and producer of television commercials, documentaries and motion picture previews. His poetry and photography have been seen in various journals including *The November 3rd Club, The Chiron Review, KCET's Departures: Poetry L.A. Style, Palabra* and his chapbook *Hitchhiking with the Guilty*.

Joelle Hannah has been writing and performing poetry since 2005. She published her chapbook *I'm Rich with no Money* in 2008. Joelle has performed in various venues throughout Ventura and Los Angeles Counties, including Hollywood Book Fair, Artist Union Gallery, and Pat Pincus Poetry Festival.

Kristoffer Huelgas is a Los Angeles poet. He spends most of his time parked on a side street in the San Fernando Valley writing poetry. He currently resides in Sun Valley, CA where he considers himself laureate.

Elizabeth Iannaci is a widely published and anthologized Los Angeles-based poet who mistrusts men who keep their hats on in the house. She earned her MFA in Poetry from the Vermont College of Fine Arts and recently was a finalist for the 2009 New Letters Literary Award. She served for five years as co-director of the Valley Contemporary Poets, has appeared at countless venues in the United States, Slovenia, and Paris, France, has one son and prefers paisley to polka dots. You would like her.

Ruth Nolan lives in Palm Desert and teaches at College of the Desert. Her poetry has appeared in *New California Writing 2011* (Heyday); *scent of rain*; *Inlandia: A Literary Journal*; *San Diego Poetry Annual 2011*; and *Raven and Crow*. She edits *Phantom Seed: A Journal of California Desert Noir*.

Allen Ginsberg said "**Marc Olmsted** inherited Burroughs' scientific nerve & Kerouac's movie-minded line nailed down with gold eyebeam in San Francisco." Olmsted teaches the on-line course *Writing Kerouac/Sitting Buddha: Spontaneous Poetics & Big Mind* at Writers.com . His book, *What Use Am I A Hungry Ghost? - Poems from 3-Year Retreat* (VCP Press, 2001), has an introduction by Ginsberg.

Angela Peñaredondo is an emerging Los Angeles poet and visual artist. She was born in Iloilo City, Philippines and grew up in Los Angeles and San Francisco areas. She received her BFA from San Francisco State University and also studied mixed media arts in the Queensland College of Art in Brisbane, Australia. She was awarded a UCLA Community Access Scholarship for poetry and a Fishtrap Fellowship.

Douglas Richardson is the author of a novel, *The Corruption of Zachary R.*, and four books of poetry, *Ghosts in Time and Space*, *Poems for Loners*, *Sugar Fish*, and *Out in the Cold, Cold Day*.

Anthony Seidman resides in the gritty and noir North Hollywood area of the San Fernando Valley. Vacant lots, motels, Pentecostal churches, Salvadoran eateries, *fichera* bars and train tracks criss-cross through the boulevards. He recently wrote about this in his collection *Combustions* (March Street Press).

Wanda VanHoy Smith is a Redondo Beach poet who reads most Tuesdays at Coffee Cartel. She has been published in several anthologies such as *poetivdiversity*, *Beyond the Valley of Contemporary Poets*, *San Gabriel Valley Poetry Quarterly*, *The Northridge Review* and most recently a book on parenting called *Because I said So*. She has been a featured reader at venues such as Coffee Cartel, Beyond Baroque, the Cafe Alibi and The San Pedro Library.

Eric Steineger teaches English Composition at A-B Tech in Asheville, North Carolina. His work has been featured in *Poetry Midwest, The Splinter Generation,* and is forthcoming in *Asheville Poetry Review.* He worked as an actor in Los Angeles for several years before moving east in 2010.

Kevin Patrick Sullivan has published two collections of poetry, *First Sight,* Mille Grazie Press,1994 and *The Space Between Things,* DeerTree Press, 2008. He's a past Poet Laureate of San Luis Obispo and curator for the Annual San Luis Obispo Poetry Festival/ Corners of the Mouth since 1984.

Eric Tuazon is an LA native. He has published several poems and short stories, and has been involved in several writers' workshops. He currently resides in Ojai and teaches English.

Mehnaz Turner was born in Pakistan and raised in southern California. She is a 2009 PEN USA Emerging Voices Fellow in Poetry. Her short story, "The Alphabet Workbook", appeared in the August 2010 issue of *Ellery Queen Mystery Magazine.* Her poems have appeared or are forthcoming in publications such as *The Journal of Pakistan Studies, Cahoots Magazine, The Pedestal Magazine,* and *An Anthology of California Poets.* An English teacher, she lives in southern California. Her chapbook, *Tongue-tied,* is forthcoming from Finishing Line Press.

Wyatt Underwood was born in New Mexico and spent his childhood in Brasil then returned to New Mexico for his teens and college. He writes poems about the world he loves and has loved: motorcycling, the desert, the mountains, the forest, the beach, sometimes the city - oh, and about women.

Florence Weinberger is a two-time Pushcart Prize nominee, award winning poet, and the author of four collections of poetry, *The Invisible Telling Its Shape* (Fithian Press,1997), *Breathing Like a Jew* (Chicory Blue Press, 1997), *Carnal Fragrance* (Red Hen Press, 2004), and *Sacred Graffiti* (Tebot Bach, 2010.) She has worked as a teacher, legal investigator, consumer advocate, and a volunteer for the Shanti Foundation.

Acknowledgements

Suzanne Lummis' Noir Metropolis quote originally appeared in the L.A. Weekly.

"Bakersfield" and "A New Town" are from Douglas Richardson's book Ghosts in Time and Space.

Brendan Constantine's poem "Panorama City" first appeared in the chapbook Antenna (1997 Past Modern Press)

Cover design includes photos by Elvis Santana (Hialeah, FL), Peter Suneson (Norrköping, Sweden) and Thomas Picard (Brooklyn, NY)

www.ingramcontent.com/pod-product-compliance
Lightning Source LLC
Chambersburg PA
CBHW072037060426
42449CB00010BA/2306